OUTSMARTING THE

ONLINE SCAMMER

AN EXCLUSIVE EXPOSITION OF ONLINE

SCAM GIMMICKS

OLUWAFEMI   EBENEZER

COPYRIGHT PAGE

DEDICATION

I dedicate this book to the Almighty God,

the creator of heavens, and the earth.

TABLE OF CONTENTS

INTRODUCTION

Even if you haven't been a victim of internet fraud, I believe you must have heard cases of them. It is a fact that internet fraud has become so ubiquitous that barely can a day pass without an incident or more reported.

Being aware of their gimmicks, modus operandi, and route of operation puts you in a better position to identify, avoid, resist, and avert their potential threat.

This exposition is expected to serve as an eye-opener and an educative piece to enlighten everyone on how these individuals called internet fraudsters, or scammers operate. You'll get to know who exactly they are in reality, how they get in contact with their prospective victims, you'll become fully aware of the methods they adopt to get their victims into submission, and finally you be given sufficient and practical steps to detect a potential threat of cyber/internet fraud.

If you've fallen prey to their bait, it doesn't make you smarter because if you don't understand how they had managed to siphon some funds from you, you are still susceptible to more financial losses.

This book exposed the activities of these fraudsters, using specifically a region of the Africa Continent-*West Africa* as the case study due to the rampant and excessively rapid rate of growth of this malicious and highly antisocial human behaviour. It is not intended to soil or denigrate the integrity of the African region mentioned above, but it's basically to educate the victims and potential victims of internet fraud and to prevent them from future threats and occurrence of such misfortune. I know it's certainly not going to be a good read for individuals in the act as it is a threat to their survival, but I have to reveal those unknown secrets to the world.

All information and expositions are carefully and painstakingly gathered from the fraudsters through proper and detailed surveillance of their activities. I had to undergo intensive training to gather this information, but I instead opt to share these gimmicks to the world than exploring them as initially intended.

CHAPTER ONE: THE

GENESIS OF

CYBER/INTERNET FRAUD.

Fraud is as old as man; internet fraud is a new generation of fraud as it involves the use of the internet to scam someone. It's quite effortless as it doesn't require the physical presence of the victims. According to the FBI's 2017 Internet Crime Report, the Internet Crime Complaint Centre (IC3) received about 300,000 complaints in which the victims lost over $1.4 billion in online fraud in just 2017. Notably, it was initially conducted over fax and traditional mail but is now done over the internet. The very first instance of a cybercrime can't be traced to a particular event. The evolution of cybercrime can be traced to the first significant attack on a digital network. As far back as 1973, a teller at a local New York bank used a computer to embezzle over $2 million.

In 1997, the FBI reported that over 85% of US companies had been hacked, surprisingly most don't even know about it. The Chaos Computer Club hacked Quicken software and can make financial transfers without the bank or the account holder awareness. Let's examine another incident in 2002; Shadow Crew's website was launched; the website was a forum and message board for hackers. On this website, members could post, learn, and share how to commit diverse forms of cyber-crimes and the antics to avoid capture. The site lasted for two years and was subsequently shut down, which led to the arrest of 28 people in the US and six other countries of the world.

As the evolution of internet technology heightened, more cases of internet/cyber-crimes began to surface and culminated. In 2007, the instances of hacking, data theft, and malware infections were on a continuous increase. The numbers of stolen records through hacking, machines infected rose into millions, the amount of damages caused projected into billions. During this period, the Chinese Government was being accused of hacking into the US and other governmental systems. In 2015, Chinese hackers stole the personal data of at least 4 million former and current government workers in one of the most significant breaches of a U.S.

government computer network ever. These are some of the substantial proofs that cybercrime has been latently penetrating the economy.

In Nigeria, this act of internet fraud became much more accessible and known few years back. It was done secretly some ten years back but has gained much popularity amongst youths and even teenagers as young as 14. Surprisingly, at the moment, children are also looking forward to becoming prominent internet fraudsters in the future as the extravagant lifestyles of successful internet fraudsters are so conspicuous and enviable.

During the early '80s and the '90s in Nigeria, the typical type of fraud is popularly termed '419'. It was believed that people with extreme intelligence and evasive abilities are a good fit for this business. It involves any tricky form of scamming someone; usually, it comes with disguising under a fake identity of a prominent figure with convincing proofs of ownership of a property. It was internalized, but as soon as a global communication system through technological advancement stepped in, the idea of scamming the whites through fax and mail came in the picture.

With the invention of e-mail in the early '90s, it was quite easy to communicate effectively and faster with their proposed victim. Due to very limited internet facilities, network providers, difficulties in accessing a cyber café; just a few who have graduated from using fax system or have been in the internalized fraud business were aware and open to the idea of using the email to communicate with foreigners in order to present a business offer or deal to them. After the victim must have gained so much trust in them through proofs and evidence of authenticity, they are made to make payment. Off they go!! You've just been scammed.

CHAPTER TWO:

SUSCEPTIBILITY TO

INTERNET FRAUD

Do you know that Americans are usually the target of these fraudsters? Do you know why? I'll explain in the next few lines. The US dollar exchange rate to most countries in Africa is usually a big deal. 1 US dollar is equivalent to about 600 XOF (West African Franc). $100 US dollars can buy a good number of wears and still some amount to keep. Unfortunately, most youths who are graduates don't even get up to $100 as monthly salary; the situation of employment has lured so many young people into this fast and growing means of making money.

Imagine a fraudster getting $20,000 from a victim, and it's enough to build a bungalow house and even get a car and still some amount of money to keep for other things in some parts of West Africa. Therefore, the target is usually foreigners, mostly Americans.

Over the past 20 years, mobile phones were acquired by the wealthy and well to do individuals who were using it basically for businesses. After another ten years, phones and sim cards became affordable that any working-class can acquire. After another five years, it became so rampant that hardly will you find an adult who doesn't have one, be it a cybercrime or not. The ubiquity of phones and related technological devices and affordable internet facilities has made it very easy to reach out to people all over the world.

The truth remains that, no one will scam you through the internet if you don't give/ create an enabling platform for it. Let's examine some of the reasons why we fall prey to these fraudsters.

1. Loneliness

When you're lonely or battling with heartbreak, they perceive it an excellent time to come into your life as a savior. They pretend as they care, they want to be as friendly as suppose, they want you to trust them. They quickly have their way around lonely people. It's much easier to persuade a solitary person, most especially in a romantic relationship.

2   Greed

I don't think anyone would admit that they are greedy. But we've got a lot of greedy people. When you have $5, and you are looking for every possible means to make it $20 within a short period without stress, it is greed. Many people get scammed as they are trying to jump into bumper offers. Imagine seeing a link that states: "Invest $200 and get $2,000 in 5 days, at the comfort of your room ". You should know you shouldn't delve into things like that if you are not greedy. No wonder you receive some unnecessary mails, you've registered and put your details on so many sites that could be detrimental to your privacy. I could remember an app that was designed by a hacker. It was a mobile recharge app; the offer that came along with the app was sumptuous. It's like saying install an app for free, use your credit card to recharge a minimum of $50 for the first time and get a bonus of $1,000 worth of airtime. It's fascinating right? You can accumulate as much as $50,000 worth of airtime by referring 50 more persons. You can see the deal looks very attractive, but it will attract only a greedy person. The promo ended when people realized their credit cards information had been obtained and you know what the rest of story is. Think deeply about any offer you're delving into; it could be a death trap. To be on a safer side, avoid them completely as they might harm you.

3. Testing syndrome

Some are inclined to always learning new things or wanting to know where an event will end. They love exploring so much. Even when you tell them something is wrong, they have this urge of trying it out to know how bad it is. People in this category usually fall prey to internet fraudsters, but in the long run, they become more knowledgeable and alert.

4. Addiction to the use of the internet.

Oh! Internet fraudsters like a very active internet user who replies messages as soon as they receive it. Slow or delayed responses usually piss them off, and hence they tend to seek another client.

Quick note: The prospective victim or a victim is usually termed, Client.

But that is not enough to make them step aside. You aren't their only target at any point in time. They could connect with over 20 prospective victims at a time, 13 might decide to ignore the request or respond to the first message while seven might respond, of which 1 or 2 might be the eventual victims. So it's quite some hard work. The longer you spend on the use of the internet and social media activities, the higher the risk of being scammed.

5. Flamboyance on social media

This is a crucial one. I see some people's update on social media, and I shake my head in pity. Out of ignorance, you see people updating status of their plans, movement, and possessions. This is usually an attraction to fraudsters. Most scams via social media platforms begin with the scammer checking through random profile pictures and details. Do you know to have too many photos can even be harmful to you? Your profile pictures can be downloaded and use to open another account by a fraudster who will then use it to scam someone using your identity. Doesn't that look, incriminating? An internet fraudster will assess your profile details on social media platforms to get an inkling of your estimated worth. When you add too many information about yourself on social media for public visibility then you're more susceptible to internet fraud. Beware!

6. Oblivious of details

Unfortunately, some have become victims of avoidable fraud cases due to their impatience in paying attention to details. Some can't take a few seconds or minutes to read the terms and conditions of a site they are putting up registration for. This usually entraps us sometimes, many of us are bonded by terms and conditions we are not aware of. You've granted access to some websites to share your details with third parties. When you keep registering on sites without having an in-depth understanding of the terms and conditions, you're putting yourself at risk.

Do you know you can lose your Facebook account by clicking on an external link where you will be required to log in your Facebook details again. Once you do, your account becomes compromised.

You'll know more about this in the subsequent chapters.

CHAPTER THREE: FACTS ABOUT SCAMMERS YOU NEVER KNEW

It's no longer news that online scam is ubiquitous all over the world. In every country, you will find an internet fraudster, as long as internet facilities are available. I'm writing based on my localized knowledge of the act in my region of abode. The description below is not generalized information of all internet fraudsters, but they are attributes that are pertinent to them.

1. They spend extravagantly

They can't stop flaunting their possessions; most times, they upload pictures of raw cash, gold necklaces, fleets of cars, and high-quality designer wears. Majority of them lodge in hotels for weeks, months; most hotels rely on them for their business survival. They are usually clubbers; they buy expensive wines and alcoholic drinks. When a victim has been duped of a huge sum, it often calls for an elaborate celebration.

Don't forget, every scammer has a clique they relate with, share ideas and problems with. So when a deal comes through, they celebrate the success together.

2. They are always with their cliques

When you find a teenager or young youth in the act of internet scam, they are usually far from their parent's reach. Due to the high moral standards of some parents, their children won't like to indulge in such act in their presence; therefore they would rather stay with their cliques since privacy is very needed to thrive in the business.

More to this, staying with the cliques ensures that latest information on effective applications, software, formats are provided since it's like group work. Sometimes, when a client is trying to be difficult, the scammer can seek help from his clique who in one way or the other have been in such a situation before. Cliques are very helpful.

3. Awake at night, sleep during the day.

Owing to time zone differences, there is variation in local time of countries in this region with countries in some part of Europe, America, Canada, and some other first nation countries. For instance, there's about 4-7 hours range between some regions here and some in the US. They don't engage in full-time jobs as their nocturnal activities don't give much room for day time work.

4. The majority are males while few are females.

Don't be deceived; you might think a female has scammed you through an online dating site. Guys mostly do it. Some applications tweak a masculine voice to sound feminine. Some don't even need an app to sound like a female. Just of recent, few females are launching into the acts, especially those who are dating some of these guys (scammers).

5. They are unsympathetic

One of the rules to a starter is, "Never pity your client." They are usually ruthless, and they don't mind emptying your bank accounts, all they care about is their aggrandizement of funds. Their target often is to get details of your credit card, siphon all you have in there and put you in further debts. They don't care if you die in the depression of financial loss; all they care about is the money.

6. They study and read about their client's region.

Sometimes, I call this illegal business a game for the creative. Much creativity and adept is needed to thrive in an online scam. They ensure to remain updated on things going on in their client's region of abode. This is because conversation might arise that could trigger question pertinent to present situations.

I remembered a young man sharing his experience on how he got blocked by his American client. Why? He (disguising to be a female claiming to be an American) told his online lover (the American) that he's ill. The American inquired on the nature of the ailment, and he responded, "Malaria." Immediately he was blocked, that was when the American realized that he had been played on. Why was the scammer blocked? Malaria is not pertinent to the region the scammer claimed to be from. Due to the help of Google search engine and related ones, they ensure it's on standby to do whatsoever search that needs to be done in addressing your questions. When you ask some questions, they swap to Google to get the answer before getting back to you (there will undoubtedly be delay in responses).

7. They don't need to rush you

Patience and persistence are instrumental in penetrating the heart of most victims of internet scam. For instance, If I'm going into online dating with a female profile and I know I'm a male, I won't think like a man anymore, I'll start thinking in the line of a woman to ensure I keep an effective communication. Making request too soon will raise a red flag, so I keep the conversation lively and fun until I make the client become addicted to me, it could take hours, weeks, or months but once it happens, the requests follow.

8. They give excuses

Oh, this is one aspect I can't but dwell very much on. A common attribute of online scammers from this region is that they give excuses now and then. When you say you want to meet them physically, they decline the request and then find excuses to back up their claims. When you want to make video calls; they tell you their phone front camera is bad. All these gimmicks are called FORMAT. When asking for their bank details, they tell you ITunes card is preferable. Please, note that some who have advanced in the business have pickers (the bank owner whose details you're given) in the country where their victims are.

9. There's a format for any situation

Just like I earlier mentioned, there's a format that goes with every scam. Just as there are various ways of scamming a client, same way do we have guidelines and steps to follow to achieve the projected goal. This is referred to as FORMAT. Uncreative minds that are into this business solely rely on the format as they lack flexibility and dynamism; they fail and lose their client whenever the client tries to outsmart the format.

10. Make use of sophisticated tools and software

You don't know what's going on at the other end of your conversation with a stranger. There are essential tools used for a starter; some of these tools are:

- *VPN (virtual private network)*

The primary function of this application is to hide one's IP address. Since the I.P address reveals your location, therefore an application is needed to change the location to a desired location of the scammer choice.

- *Grammarly*

A good number of these internet fraudsters aren't exceptional in the use of English language grammatical construction. Therefore they employ this application to correct their grammatical errors. Since it is known that bad and poor grammatical construction is a quick way to piss a client off, this application is no doubt a beneficial application to them.

- *Cloning application*

This application helps you to run multiple accounts of the app on a device. Don't be surprised that a scammer can have up to 20 Gmail accounts on a device without having to log out one for the other. It's a matter of cloning the application.

- *Dating application*

There are thousands of dating applications available on Playstore, Apple store, and the rest. Some of these applications ensure that users from the same location (country) are matched. The use of VPN has compromised this move. There are so many more sophisticated tools, but these are just the basics for starters.

CHAPTER FOUR: THE

DETAILS OF ONLINE

DATING SCAM

The Downside to Online Dating

There are many ways you could be scammed, and there are several formats used. I'll begin this exposition with the most common and often used method of online scam. Majority of those who are deeply rooted in internet fraud/scam started with the basic which is **online dating**. During the period of my secretive findings, a friend of mine had already made some pretty massive cash from the online scam business, which made me understand that I need to start from the primitive stage before advancing into bigger plots.

I want to magnify this scam - **ONLINE DATING SCAM.**

I am going to dwell so much of this because it's by far the most common online scam being executed by teenagers and young youths. It's straightforward to implement, all they need is their mobile phone if the laptop isn't available and active and steady internet service.

First, the scammer decides on the gender to use, and it could be a black man pretending to be a white man or a white woman depending on whether he wants a male or female client. The truth is that the two are done simultaneously; a starter will be urged to open both a male and a female account on a dating site and in the long run might stick to a more favorable one.

The Male Account

The male account is not as common as the female profile. This process begins with the scammer going on any social media platform to view and download sufficient profile pictures of any white man, preferably a handsome young man. You remember I mentioned the need to be careful about how we display everything about ourselves on social media. Your images could be what a scammer here is using for various dubious acts. Social media sites like Facebook, Instagram, Twitter, etc. allows users to download uploaded pictures of other users. Once the photo album is created, the scammer creates a new profile account on whichever chat/dating platform they want to use. The scammer now will be on the lookout for white women, especially those in the age range of 45 and above who are divorced, widowed or single tending to fall in love again.

Most times for the male account, a military profile is usually used to win the heart of those women. It is perceived that most white women around 40 years upward love military men as they are guaranteed of extra protection. It is not a generalized percept or a fact, but that's their thoughts here.

The conversation

The conversation usually begins with some few lines like a letter of introduction. Since it's a format, the naive ones (scammers) try to follow the format of the conversation strictly, and when stuck with some questions, they consult more experienced colleagues for help on how to respond to issues that are outside the laid out format. When chatting with them and such scenario comes up, they quickly connect with clique members for help after which they get back to you with a response.

The Female Account

This is very common; this is known to pay much quickly. It's easy for a man to fall in love with what they see. Just the same way a male account is made, a female account takes same shape. The scammer goes to a random female profile page (Facebook, Instagram, and other dating sites), downloads her uploaded pictures (usually all of her photographs if possible to convince the client). Often, a scammer won't use someone profile with little pictures; they ensure the user profile page has many images so they won't run out of stock whenever their clients demand photos. Due to the fact that some white men love seeing nude pictures of females they having an online date with; this prompts these scammers to be good followers of porn stars on the social media and some paid sites in order to access the nude pictures of these porn stars which in turn is presented to their clients when demanded. Scammers search for their potential victims on dating sites like eharmony, OkCupid, livedatematch and so many more. Once a client is gotten on any of these dating sites, the scammer tries to move the conversation to another platform such as Google hangouts for quicker accessibility and notification of messages from their clients. This might be a red flag.

Other things you need to know:

1. They won't ask you for a gift or any material things from the inception. They want to earn your trust first. That's the motive. They want to create an impression in you that they are not after your money but the love. This will make you vulnerable and susceptible to their plots.

2. They could send you a gift first
There's no better way to earn your trust than sending you a gift prior to you sending anything to them. This is to make you think they are genuine about their love for you.

3. They give excuses
One thing they try to avoid seriously is when you bring up talks of meeting in person. Another thing is video calls; they

always find an excuse like they have got a faulty front camera. They will lure you to sending them a phone if you really want a video call with them. After sending the phone, you're blocked; you won't hear from them again.

4. They don't request for Gift cards from the inception, later they could ask for more significant sum through transfer medium such as Wire Transfer, Western Union, etc. They usually use pickers to receive these funds. There is more about a picker in chapter seven.

How to Outsmart Online Dating Scam

Usually, a scammer won't ask you for anything in the first few weeks of conversation; this is to make you feel they aren't after your money. When you become attached, they begin to request for gift cards. An Amazon or iTunes gift card of $100 is enough to buy some good wears and even enough to drink some bottles of beer in this region. Imagine a scammer having three to five clients paying $200 weekly; it's a big hit. When they tired of asking for gift cards, they try to get your credit card details to rake a more significant fund from you. This is a red flag!

The following are tips to avoid being scammed on online dating:

- Try to avoid profile of individuals who are too far from your present location on dating sites. They must be in an area that you can quickly hook up to meet. Don't get too deep into a conversation before arranging your first meeting; it could make you so vulnerable to an online dating scam.

- In cases where you meet someone on a dating date, and they are very swift to suggesting you move the conversation to another chat platform like hangouts or Facebook; be alert, it is possibly a scam.

- Don't try to play along with scammer online. Don't hesitate to press the BLOCK button when you suspect any activity associated with a scam. You might be a victim of another act if you are perceived as a stubborn client.

- A new Facebook profile of a user tells you the account has been purposely designed to scam people. Facebook usually block such accounts; this is why these scammers hack into people's Facebook accounts as Facebook hardly block an existing account that has been in existence for some years.

- Try as much as you can to avoid online dating site. Scammers have taken over the place; they even pay for premium packages on these sites so they can look legit and visible. The more you are addicted to these sites, the more susceptible you are.

- You don't have to be deceived on dating sites. When you call for a meeting and the so-called HE/SHE is refusing to see you; that's a red flag. Be smart, don't be too carried away with a prolonged conversation that could make you lose your emotional grip, if not you will find yourself sending iTunes cards, Amazon cards, and even sharing your credit card details with a stranger you haven't seen in person.

CHAPTER FIVE: THE GIFT

CARD SCAM

Gift cards are the fastest and the easiest way to cash out money from a client. Once a gift card is sent from a client, the scammer sends the image as sent by the client to a website where they will be sold at a much lower rate to the original value of the card. For instance, if you put up a $100 US iTunes card on a site such as paxful.com, you will see buyers online who will state their buying price. Once you are cool with a price, you'll have a chat with the buyer (Note: There are cases of scam on those sites too). During the conversation with the buyer on the exchange site, the card will be sent to the buyer who will confirm that the gift details has been received, after that the buyer sends the seller the Bitcoin equivalence of the card at the agreed rate. A buyer can buy at $0.6, which means you will get a value of $60 on a card of $100. The Bitcoin equivalence is sold to get the local currency equivalence.

Like I mentioned in the previous chapter, most online scammers on dating site request for gift cards(which could be sold online to get the local currency equivalence) since it is untraceable, unlike bank funds transfer. When they are about to pounce on you massively, they lure you to sending your credit card details. But aside requesting for the gift card directly from a client, there are other ways victims are made to send a meaningful amount of gift card. Read below for more:

How the iTunes Gift Card Scam Works

These scammers use the iTunes gift card to siphon some funds from the victims. The continuous occurrence of this act prompted Apple to release the statement below on their site to keep its users on alert.

"iTunes Gift Cards are solely for the purchase of goods and services on the iTunes Store and App Store. Should you receive a request for payment using iTunes Gift Cards outside of iTunes and the App Store please reports it at ftc.gov/complaint."

This begins with the scammer trying to persuade their victims to purchase gift cards. When the victims eventually succumb to this persuasion, they proceed to the purchase of the iTunes gift card either online or in a store. They then mail the code on the card to the scammer, who subsequently drains whatever value the gift card has got, or trade it in exchange for Bitcoins which can be converted into the local currency equivalence.

One of the newer methods used involves a scammer impersonating an Internal Revenue Service Agent, convincing their victims to pay their taxes over the phone using iTunes gift cards. This should raise a red flag.

It doesn't have to be iTunes cards; there are many other gift cards that can serve the same purpose as iTunes cards, as much as they have monetary value and can quickly be sold. The America iTunes card is the easiest to sell gift card online. Other gift cards include; Amazon gift cards, PayPal, (Reloadable cards like Vanilla, Money Pack, etc.). Since Wire service (a means of transferring funds) has become quite challenging to use as a result of the victims heeding to warnings on Wire transfers. Therefore scammers have decided to opt for iTunes card scam as the new method of payment. Contrary to the wire service, iTunes card scam is difficult to trace. When the card is sent, it is irreversible.

Gift Card Scam Red Flag /Tips to Avoid Scam

- Purchase your gift cards only from stores. They could tell you they are selling a bulky quantity of gift cards at a lower price.

- Don't send a gift card to a stranger; it could be an open door for bigger plots against you.

- Ignore any call or text from any security, tax, bank agent requesting you to pay for a bill or levy through gift card. It's a big scam. Go to their office to make a payment or through their official bank account if at all you must do so.

CHAPTER SIX: THE CREDIT CARD SCAM.

Falling a victim of a credit card scam is something you don't want to experience. Whether you've been a victim before or not, you can be the next victim if you don't know how your credit card details can be obtained illegally. I'll discuss some of the ways your credit card details can be obtained illegally with or without you giving it out.

A credit card, unlike a debit card, enables a scammer to make purchases with or without money in it, and that's why it is always a target. The more exposed you are about this scam, the less susceptible and vulnerable you are to this scam. There are various ways your credit card details can be obtained from you with or without your consent. Most online dating scam usually terminates when the scammer gets their client's credit card details. Other ways in which you can become a victim of a credit card scam is discussed below:

1. A Phishing Website

You might be wondering what a phishing website is; it is a fake website that looks like its original one. For example, everyone is familiar with www.facebook.com, but I can create a phishing website that looks exactly like the original Facebook site, but it will be something like www.faacebook.com, which you might hardly notice that there's a difference in the web address compared to the original.

So clicking on such site, you might think you are on the original and intended site.

Now you have an understanding of what a phishing website is; this is where the scam comes in. Usually, they create a website with an e-commerce platform where you can purchase items online, which are generally very cheap as compared their original prices in other online platforms. For instance, you might see a link that will redirect you to Amazon to purchase an item at an extremely cheap rate. If you hurriedly click without checking the website meticulously, you might fall a victim. The reason is that the website will look similar to www.amazon.com; it could be something like www.amazoon.com. Since the website will be designed like the original Amazon site, you might not know you are heading towards trouble. A phishing website is specially designed by website designers who are into hacking as well. Note that any information you provide on the website such as login details, profile info, and card details will be visible to the administrator of the phishing website. So can you perceive danger?

Again, it could be a fake Bitcoin website willing to sell their Bitcoins at a reasonable amount. Interested individuals will be made to purchase using their credit card. Once you input your credit card details, the details can be collected and used for whatsoever purpose the fraudster intends.

2. Phone call format

Don't be surprised that a scammer from this part of the world can put a call through to someone in the US through some applications that grant US phone numbers to anyone anywhere in the world.

This privilege is explored in this trick I'm able to share.

A scammer needs your full name as written on your card, card number, and card name to put this trick into play. Next, you receive a call from someone with an American accent stating their badge number (a fake one) and claiming to be from the security and fraud department of a credit card company. Having stated your card number and name, you might be more than convinced to think it's not a scam. The next trick is to make you answer your security questions. Questions such as;

* What is the name of your first pet?

*Where did you spend your childhood?

* What's your mother's maiden name?

These questions aren't important; they are just a way of showing concern and willingness to help to the client. Lastly, you will be asked to supply your CVC number using a format (trick) which could look like this:

"To ascertain your ownership of this card, can you confirm the last three digits at the back of your ATM card?"

Once you give the correct digits away, your card becomes utterly vulnerable to theft; you've just handed the key to them (scammer).

Account Hacking through Phishing

I'll dwell more on how scammers use phishing on social media in this section. I have explained the foundation of phishing earlier in this chapter. Apart from scammers obtaining your credit card details through phishing, phishing can be used to get your personal information, confidential information about you which can be used to process a bigger scam. Here, I'll expose how your Facebook account can be hacked through a phishing website.

When you are on Facebook, you would have seen external links with attractive headlines of promotions, false breaking news, pornographic pictures/videos or anything that could lure you into clicking the link to read further. When you click this link, you aren't hacked yet; you'll be required to log in your Facebook details to continue. Immediately you drop these details to a similar-looking Facebook login page, your login information would have been dropped to the initiator of the phishing. The scammer logs into your Facebook account with the acquired details, and change the login details to deny you the accessibility to your account. At this point, the account is no longer yours. Now your account has been hacked, and anything could be going on behind you.

Once the scammer logs into your account, they start sending messages to your friends making requests such as Gift cards or even requesting for their card details for something urgent. The previous conversations with your friends' guide them in creating a convincing event to enable them get whatsoever they need. Remember that not all of your friends will place a call through to you to confirm if it is actually you or not making the request.

I used Facebook as an instance; this scam isn't limited to Facebook alone. Be careful with websites that require your login details so that you won't be the next victim of credit card scam or account hack and other related unpleasant events.

CHAPTER SEVEN: OTHER FORMATS USED/TIPS FOR STAYING SAFE

- The Grant Format

This is very common in the recent time. How do they go about this? It begins with getting a formidable profile. Some go the extent of creating a profile with celebrity profile information.

Next, they message random users telling them that they just received a grant from the government. It's usually a massive amount of dollars. Mind you; proofs will be shown if you show interest in the offer.

If your responses are forthcoming, the stage continues advancing. You'll be made to pay a sum into an account (A picker account).

I'll digress a bit to explain who a picker is.

A picker is someone whose bank account is used to receive money from the victim; then the picker transfers the money to the scammer after which he must have taken his commission. Most pickers are from the country of the victim).

If you tell the scammer that you don't have the money to apply for the grant, you'll be persuaded to sign some documents stating that you want the grant, but you aren't financially capable to pay for the application. At this point, if you don't flee, you'll be in for another drama. After some time, the scammer will start bringing up some unpleasant, tense and scary updates such as the FBI has hijacked the process and it is trouble for you both. You'll be shown the documents you signed and with a stamp that they are in the FBI custody. The scammer will use this to make you fret so you can pay some amount to avoid having a case with the FBI. You'll continue paying until you realize you are running without being chased.

Safety Tip: To avoid being scammed through this format, don't sign any document or pay any amount to a stranger, if there is any grant, go to their official office address to make inquires.

▪ Sextortion

The victim is lured into sharing intimate videos and images. This usually occurs on dating sites. The scammer won't make any request from the outset; they only want you to perform some explicit sexual acts and send to them with your face shown. When the scammer has gotten sufficient nude pictures and videos of their victims, they threaten their victims to release the pictures and videos online or to other sources that could put their identity at stake.

Safety Tip: Intimate stuff or affairs should be done with someone you have a good knowledge of, not a stranger. If you are a victim of such, block off any communication with the threatener, I think this helps a lot.

▪ Hitman Scam

This is one of the reasons why it is wise to keep the information provided on social media page minimal to avoid supplying information to the hands of those that will use it against you. This scam involves terrifying threats of physical violence or death, which is usually sent through text messages but mostly through mail. The sender of the mail claims to be a person hired to terminate your life and will offer to relinquish their role if you can pay a fee. The message might include personal details about you which are usually gotten from your social media profile and other possible sources online; this makes the threat looks more scaring and genuine.

Safety Tip: This kind of mail or message can be quite worrisome that will leave you in a trepid state, but shouldn't make you fret so much that will you make a fund transfer hastily without engaging the police.

- **Terrorist Threat Scam**

All a scammer needs to do is to be updated on international news, as soon as news pops in regarding any terrorist attack or threat in any region of the world; they cease this privilege to contact some citizens of such country/region making threats of a massive terrorist attack in their locality. The scammer will then offer to spare the potential victim's life and family's if they pay up the required sum.

<u>Safety Tip</u>: Cases like this should be reported to the security agents. Don't engage in any conversation with the mail sender before notifying the appropriate security personnel.

- **Bomb Threat Scam**

Similar to the one mentioned above, this capitalizes on an event related to bomb attack or threatening notice. A scammer targets people in this region and this is one of the reasons why these fraudsters are always updated and interested in international news especially those involving bomb attacks and threats. This is a time for them to make some cash out of the situation. Usually they send an email telling people that there is a bomb planted in their building and can only be disconnected only if a specific fee is paid.

▪ Ghost Realtor Trick

This is another trick that is adopted by those who feel online dating isn't paying them as much as they want. This fraudulent act is termed *"ghost realtor trick."* The scammer pretends to be a realtor (a person or business that sells or leases out real estate, acting as an agent for the property owner) and uploads pictures of a luxurious apartment for sale or rent which usually look much cheaper than the real market value. When the victim comes across the uploaded photographs and expresses interest in purchasing the apartment/property, and then proceeds to the payment of a huge amount of money into the realtor's account, the realtor blocks off the communication link, and that is the end. Making a fake document for a property isn't something difficult to do; samples are online.

<u>Safety Tip</u>: So don't be tricked into paying a huge amount for a property you haven't seen and made concrete findings on.

▪ Job Offer Scam

When you are desperately in need of a job, you're most vulnerable to this sort of scam. A scammer will research a company's details and design a format that will convince their prospective client. Mails are sent to random users alerting them of job offers. Once you express interest, you will be made to fill in your personal information to proceed with the process through the provided link. Meanwhile, your profile information provided could be used to scam you in some other ways. At a point, you will be instructed to pay a fee to process your application which could be a small amount but mind you; you aren't the only target. The small processing fee might mean a little to you, but with many victims, it's a big hit. Note that the job scam isn't always about getting money from you; it is always targeted towards getting vital profile information about you, which will subsequently be used to defraud you in other ways. This is why you will receive some emails and calls from a stranger stating your full details, impersonating a government agency. A job scam registration portal is one of the ways they get your information.

<u>Safety Tip</u>: Don't hastily give away your information all in the name of registration. When companies are recruiting, ensure you go to their official websites for more enquires, or you contact an insider in the organisation if you have any. Don't pay or compensate anyone online for a job you haven't gotten. Don't be lured into paying before getting a job. It's a red flag.

- Cancelled Account

When you receive a notification of an account cancellation or suspension, you could fret especially when it's an important account. How will a scammer know you have an account with a company? Most times it's a trial by error. I can assume you have a Netflix account since it's popular. If an account suspension message is sent to

10 persons, it might apply to 5-6 persons, and 2 or 3 could respond.

Some scammers spend time creating official-looking emails from reputable service providers. The target is notified of an imminent account suspension and that they need to provide information to keep it open. The email might include a link to a phishing site requesting login credentials and billing details to secure the "continuation of service."

The information collected is enough to siphon a large amount of money from the victim, and in rare cases, you might be asked to pay directly through Gift cards or into an account which will be received through a picker who will extend the money to the scammer.

Safety Tip: If you haven't violated the terms and conditions of use, your account can't be terminated. When you receive such notification, don't respond. That's the solution.

▪ Scam Compensation Scam

Sounds funny! But you might have seen a mail usually found in the spam folder stating that your name is listed in a scam compensation list and their company is coordinating a compensation program for scam victims. Whether you've been a victim or not, it's a scam, and you shouldn't be moved by it. You'll be required to provide some personal information to start claiming your compensation. Don't proceed to supply any further information; it can come back to haunt you.

Safety Tip: No one will compensate you for being scammed, don't be deceived. You are heading for more losses if you yield or show interest in this kind of compensation scheme.

CHAPTER EIGHT: WHEN TO FLEE/ PRECAUTIONARY MEASURES (DETECTION)

Detecting an online scam can be quite easy as well as technical. There are new tricks and gimmicks popping up every day; therefore, it's difficult to predict a rigid pattern of their operations. Online dating is soon becoming obsolete as it's becoming rampant and this has brought many into awareness and alertness. Bear in mind that the more you become aware of their gimmicks, the more they dig into new ideas to trick their potential victims. The truth is that you have to develop some protective mechanisms against their plots.

No matter how smart you can be, you can be outsmarted by an experienced scammer if you are not updated on trending scam tricks. More and more of these gimmicks will be revealed as the event unfolds. I'll discuss how you can easily detect a scam in a glance and how to avoid being a victim.

A. The online dating

The truth is you can avoid online dating or any form of a blind date. The more you are addicted to online dating, the more susceptible and vulnerable you are to internet scam and fraud.

If you insist on keeping up with the act, here are the tips that can guide you against being scammed.

* Depending on the dating platform you find yourself, always look out for the profile pictures of your proposed lover. Try to check them on other social media platforms if they exist. Anyone telling you they are not on any other social media platform aside the dating site you hooked up is probably telling you lies, they will even tell you they are abstaining from them (social media) because they have been scammed in the past all to earn your pity. Observe the uploaded pictures, and if you discover that they were recently uploaded, there is a tendency that the account was created purposely to scam. It isn't always the case, but that should arouse your curiosity and alertness.

* Are you dating someone who doesn't want to see you but wants your money? Then it's nothing other than a scam.

Scammers are very good lairs; they find a way to avoid things that could expose their real identity. They try to avoid videos call most times. The secret of getting them is this; check their profile picture used, initiate a video call to counter check and verify that they are the same. But the truth is that a scammer would rather avoid you when they discover you're a difficult nut to crack.

B. Phishing

Phishing is done mostly by scammers who have graduated from online dating scam as it is perceived to have a perspective of yielding more funds and within a short period. You can avoid being a victim of phishing, although it can be challenging to detect. Following the tips below, you will most likely avoid being a victim to phishing. If you're not sure a website is legit, there are quick and easy ways to check you aren't risking your personal and financial information. Here are ways to check if a website is legit.

1. Look closely at the content presentation of the website

When you look closely at a fake and phishing website, you can easily detect a flaw if you pay close attention. There are apparent and conspicuous errors/flaws which could be in spellings, grammatical construction, or graphics design quality. Although fake and phishing websites can be tricky to spot, as they are often almost identical to the original website.

Example:
Subject: Your Amazon.com order cannot be shipped

Hello,There was a problem processing your order. You will not be able to access your account or place orders with us until we confirm your information.click here to confirm your account.We ask that you not open new accounts as any order you place may be delayed.

For more details, read our Amazon Prime Terms & Conditions.

Sincerely,

Amazon.com.au

© Amazon.com.au, Inc. or its affiliates. All rights reserved. Amazon, Amazon.com, the Amazon.com logo, Prime and Amazon Prime are trademarks of Amazon.com, Inc

Below is an example of a phishing mail of Amazon

Note: The site you are expected to drop your details is Amazon.com.au

The *.au* makes it different from the original site, and it is a phishing website.

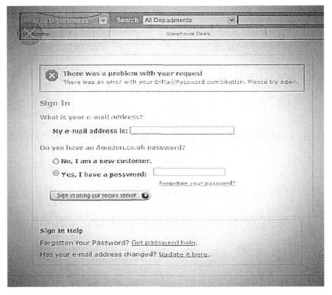

Below is an example of a phishing website that collects your information

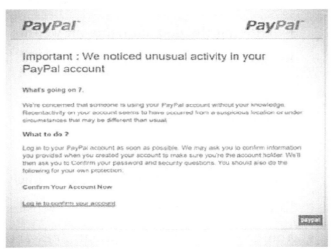

This is a phishing email using a PayPal

2. Find out who owns the web domain of the website you're surfing

All domains have to register their web address or URL, so it's important to check who has registered the web domain or URL of the website. This will help you identify the authenticity of the website as you will get to know the name of the company responsible for the domain (how reputable they are will give you more assurance). You can check for the details by entering the domain name on websites like whois.net.

3. Contact them directly

A legitimate company usually include their contact information including a publicly listed telephone number on their website. You can check their telephone lines and put a call through if the phone number goes through to a business line, that's a good sign but a mobile number or no answer during office hours is more suspicious, and with that you need to be cautious. If you want to dig further, you need to check out the history of the provided telephone number using websites like Whocallsme.

4. Check the https:// details

This is one of the things internet users don't pay attention to. Visiting a website that asks you for personal information or login details without redirecting you to an https:// connection, you're advised to leave immediately. Whenever you visit a secure connection online, you should see a padlock symbol next to the URL toolbar to indicate you are logged on to a secure connection. When you shop online or share your details on a website (via registration), ensure you are using an https:// or secure server internet connection. This ensures that other web users can't spy on your details, for example, your credit card information.

The padlock symbol indicates a secure connection

5. Finally, you can go on site engines to search for the website you're visiting to

know if it has any negative review associated with fraud.

Finally, be careful when surfing websites (esp. popular ones). Check for the correct website address. When you receive a call stating you have tax issues or any criminal allegation, be bold enough to ask for their office address rather than settling it on the phone by making payments, it's a scam. Don't allow a foreigner to who is not in your country put you in bondage in your abode.

*****

This is very important. Please read carefully.

I have discussed reasons why young people delve into this illegal business in this part of the world; I want to discuss further an aspect of this scam that many whites don't believe in. At a point, these scammers realized that it isn't easy scamming their victims any longer as their antics are being exposed through their victims; hence they conceived that there's a need to dig deeper to find a way of hypnotizing their victims through diabolical means.

It's a severe issue here as human body parts are being used to prepare these charms. Whether you believe in hypnosis or charms or not, they exist, and they are being used to manipulate unyielding and difficult clients to releasing all they have. While I'm still gathering my information together to provide you with exclusive information on how victims of internet scams are being hypnotized using diabolical means and what it entails and how to escape such spells, remain vigilant in your use of internet and don't hesitate to block off any communication looking suspicious.

ABOUT THE AUTHOR

Oluwafemi Ebenezer is a blog writer, an educator, and a researcher. His research into the writing of this book is intended to create a global awareness on the scams and fraud associated with the use of the internet. As an agent of positive change for Africa, the author is making efforts to dissuading the teens and young youths from delving into cybercrimes as a means of livelihood.

To be notified on the release of the next book: **The effects of hypnosis in internet scam,** contact the mail: Browniemarkin2000@gmail.com

Made in the USA
Monee, IL
30 April 2022